Dolphins

Contents

Written by Fiona Undrill

Big and little dolphins

There are different sorts of dolphin.
The biggest is the orca.

Orcas are whoppers! They are bigger than elephants.

Orcas are clever. They can chat with clicks, groans and moans!

Having big, clever brains helps when
they hunt. They can plan their attack.

Hector's dolphins are little.
They are not often seen.

A Hector's dolphin is not much bigger than you!

Jumping dolphins

When dolphins jump up, they go high into the air.

The Amazon is the longest river.

Amazon river dolphins can be pink!

High-speed dolphins

With their strong tails, dolphins can whip up a good speed.

The quickest is the common dolphin,
which whizzes along much quicker than
the best runners!

Which dolphin is it?

It is big.   It is quick.   It is pink.

It jumps high.